T0121532

Ouafa and Thawra:
About a Lover From Tunisia

Poetry, drawings, essay...

Arturo Desimone

Edited by Tendai Rinos Mwanaka
Drawings by Arturo Desimone

Mwanaka Media and Publishing Pvt Ltd,
Chitungwiza Zimbabwe
*
Creativity, Wisdom and Beauty

Mwanaka Media and Publishing Pvt Ltd (*Mmap*)
24 Svosve Road, Zengeza 1
Chitungwiza Zimbabwe
mwanaka@yahoo.com
www.africanbookscollective.com/publishers/mwanaka-media-and-publishing
https://facebook.com/MwanakaMediaAndPublishing/

Distributed in and outside N. America by African Books Collective
orders@africanbookscollective.com
www.africanbookscollective.com

ISBN: 978-1-77906-487-5
EAN: 9781779064875

DISCLAIMER
All views expressed in this publication are those of the author and do not
necessarily reflect the views of *Mmap*.

iii

Acknowledgments

The following poems in the collection have previously appeared in literary journals:

About a Lover From Tunisia in the The New Orleans Review, 2013. (see the New Orleans Review webfeatures, http://www.neworleansreview.org/a-lover-from-tunisia/)

Remembering Tunisia in African Writing Magazine (issue 12, 2014)

Birds Over Mainframes in African Writing Magazine issue 12, then reprinted in the anthology Poeming Pigeons by the Poetry Box Press (Spring 2015)

OUAFA HIND in Knot-Lit Magazine, winter issue 2015

Goodbye Tunis, Aenas and Dido in The Brown Critique (New Delhi, India) 2012

Tunisian Women Activists on the blog A Tunisian Girl, 2012.

Table of Contents

"Post-Dido, drinking *kahwa* near the eternal construction site of Hotel Tannith (not liked by Tanith) in Carthage" mixed-media on paper in diary, Tunis 2012

title of drawing proposed as cover art/ on first page upon opening the book: ''Elle Dort / Dans sa Plaisir'' mixed media on paper, 2012

Introduction

After the news of Tunisia's mass-revolt broke out in 2010, I decided to visit the small North African country as soon as the opportunity came my way, in the hope of learning more about the reality of revolution. When a political organisation I knew of announced a call for delegates to attend an international conference in Tunis for independent press-workers, I signed up immediately to become a "correspondent" sending dispatches.

At that time, my knowledge about Tunisia remained limited to mostly Western references, like Paul Klee's paintings of Kairouan. The exception was a story told to me by Mr Hanagid. A Moroccan Rabbi I had met in Amsterdam, at a community centre we happened to frequent in order to receive free social-work-assistance for immigrants in the outer reaches of that city, one day as we sat in the waiting room, ritually complained for half an hour about the quality of Dutch coffee, while I nodded. Then Rabbi Sami Hanagid, my fellow maladapted newcomer to the Netherlands, told me the legend of Kaheena. A medieval Judeo-Berber queen, she had led her tribal army in Tunisia (or what later became Tunisia) against the first Islamic invaders, and almost defeated them twice; liberating her people once. It sounded epic, and quite personal for the African Rabbi marooned in Amsterdam, who shuddered in his thick black suit black and black-grey beard, retelling the story as if he had witnessed these battles unfold centuries before his birth. I never saw Mr S. Hanagid, formerly of Rabat, again, after a large modernist Mosque-edifice sponsored by Qataris sprang up in front of that community centre in the Amsterdam banlieue. Other than that scholarly (though hardly impartial) source, my Tunisian references were then mostly Western--despite my arduous study of Arabic, then in its initial phases: a dawn.

I had left my South American familiar surroundings at the age of 22, and moved to Europe. Ironically, in Europe my interest in the poetic and musical traditions, as well as the politics of North Africa and the Middle East (the MENA) bloomed, all of a sudden. There, thanks to the phenomenon of modern immigration (a process in which I also participated, since having left my creole-speaking island Aruba for the metropolis) I began to more directly encounter many political and cultural discourses surrounding the nearby Orient, as well as the ideas of Frantz Fanon.

Even back in the Caribbean and Latin America, however, one inevitably encounters reverberations and the beautiful debris of that historical 15th century sundering of Andalucía and Spain, when the Arabs and Sephardic Jewry, banished by mass-expulsions from Catholic imperial Spain, brought their fugitive culture and traditions to the then-colonised Americas, and elsewhere. Many North Africans and Middle Easterners of all religions speak as if all this happened only yesterday: a memory preserved in poetry and music, in ideologies and sermon after sermon. In Tunisia, the reference to the historical exile from Andalucia remains present and potent.

No wonder that Federico García Lorca, from the 20th century city of Granada--home to the Alhambra, "the red castle'' (Arabic *al-Ahmar* 'the Red') exerted an important influence upon Mahmoud Darwish, the Palestinian poet. Darwish, as I learned in Tunisia, had even lived out years of his exile in Tunis, very near to the house of the unnamed woman in the first poem of this collection.

The role of politics remains undeniable (and intertwined with it, love and eros: those potions and enhancers of radicalism.)

I needed to see from close-by what the political process of revolution looks like; what forces a revolution unleashes in society. As Franz Fanon knew, these liberated forces are pandemonium, and not entirely rational-- quite often to the contrary: magical, sensual, surreal.

With the Tunisian revolts of the early 21st century, the Benali and RCD-Party dictatorship in Tunisia had finally been held responsible for atrocious practices, including forced disappearances, the detention and torture of youths, and the more conventional crimes of corruption.

I had grown up marked by the legacy of the Argentine military dictatorship responsible for 30,000 disappearances of youths in my exiled father's country (my father had more-or-less fled from Argentina to the Caribbean in the late 1970s and stayed there.) The stories of detentions, disappearance and police states had made an indelible impression on me, and gave me a thirst for finally retaliating. I felt I could not quite miss the opportunity to see what happens when a population successfully overthrows a decrepit police-state, no longer fearing the secrecy of dungeons.

Since Homer, and other oral poets of that time on other continents, it has long been held that, like religion, love and eros can give enhanced powers to a combatant. Though I saw that theory confirmed in my surroundings then, I never pretended to being a combatant, even as I had hoped to find the opportunities sought for by 20th century writers who travelled to become both correspondents and active soldiers on the Spanish Republican side during the Spanish Civil War (like the youthful Orwell, or like the great Surinamese writer Albert Helman, who corresponded for a Dutch newspaper, despite his anti-imperial sympathies fired up by the Spanish revolutionaries.) I kept revisiting Tunisia, and wrote poetry, creative nonfiction, political essays, and made drawings.

The poems and drawings in this collection came about during that period of 2011-2013. With gratitude do I celebrate the publication of this collection with an African publishing house, run by a fellow poet-combatant.

Arturo Desimone
Buenos Aires, May 1 2019

About a Lover from Tunisia

I kissed her on her buttocks without the slightest shame
her name,____in Arabic
means "a river in paradise"

should I drown,
flowers will grow from her gates--
truths are just abstract flowers.

*

I have to stop thinking about a dead affair,
about a lover from Tunisia and her buttocks
and her tears,
or that buttocks might have the shape of tears

I have to stop.
I have to forget about Fridays.
I have to write my story

I have to forget about the prospects of laughter
with anyone but myself,
of alcohol cut with a knife
from the moon's belly

I have to forget about an Arab girl's
foot following the circular motion

of wine she held,

1

and kissing her dark lips in March,

on the third night of Pesach,

the first I celebrated in twenty years

*

There is a girl who I love

and who is from the village of Sidi

Bouzid near the *Jbala* mountains

of Regueb, where boys toil

in the sun singing

"C'est normal ici" their epic poem

on their motorcycles smuggling gasoline

from Libya to sell for a profit on the sidewalks.

But she has not seen this reality,

having moved from the country

to the city as a child

(her father wanted her to be good in school,

 so he built a house next to the school.)

there is a girl I love and her skin is dark,

and her hair is dark and falls

on her cheeks which are capable

of turning red through her brown.

there is a girl I love and I have kissed her

in many parts of Tunisia

in Bizerte by the sea,

in the countryside,

in the ruins of Utique

and the amusement parks of Carthage

But I have made love to her at only one location:

next to a lake by the mosque near La Marsa

where the African birds and a river go to pray

when the sun nestles like a bird in the Atlas mountains visible from_____'s balcony

The call to prayer called Salat is my cue

to kiss her and undress her

I am proud to have found a girl who lets me

undress her,

and not one who undresses herself as routine

on the first call to prayer she is already naked,

we say "good morning" and I say it again to her buttocks on the second call
to prayer she has left

on third and fourth I am writing drawing walking on fifth she lands on my
shoulder and we become children who cannot speak or make sense

*

On the other side of a mountain a black bird stood

on a wall without house.

I returned on the highway to Tunis

where she landed again on my shoulder

introduced her name: her name,

the name for a substance

of a river in paradise,

 swan of Carthage Salambo

5

I LOVE YOU BECAUSE

I love you because
you are a child
when you are being loved,
being driven--
maybe all who cupid cut
became again children.

ALL ALONG

All along thought I had been
in a cocoon,
waiting to mature, be born--
but I was already a man,
not in my cocoon
but in the web
of a great spider.

and plastic and vinex city of order,

the machine that keeps this place
up and running,
makes odd, cold sounds--
like in Byzantine Christian chants of progress,
the dirge whistled by Catullus, engineer:

the Roman realtor,
he who hated your country for its figs,
he who believed in competitors.
Tannith
 does not compete,

only mediocrity ever sought
competition
in the ruins of the Roman Circuses,
near Sidi Bousaid and in Utique.

"Le ours pauvre, Ouafa la petite algerienne riche et le serveuse très snob à Paris" drawing Paris

CONVERSATION AFTER ALARM CLOCK OF THE JEMMA MOSQUE NEXT DOOR

Talk about politics in bed,
after love,
these idiocies --
talking about Israel, oppression, white black
Why did I
let this happen,
dead birds   (a'asfouroun عصفور)
  in our mouths   as if,
                  or because,
I believed it necessary
        to say anything
at all,
after love,
when the morning is
clear golden,
murk--
I can smell soul under her scalp
when I bury my nose
in her dark raven curls.

RIGHTS.

I have the right to say 'dark raven curls'
when describing the hair
of sleeping Arab women it is written
in Shir
Ha Shirim,
Book Dalith.

my lover
from Tunisia never,
not once,
could she write
back (as long as she loved me)
in Français.

Tunis red night, obsidian-head activist Arroi holds up a bird
that clenches a scorp by the tail in its beak, the scorp gives the human girl flowers.
Stars with genitals on electric wires of Progress dangle from the blue night. She
has strong hands for a girl, from textile-pulley-machines and throwing rocks at
night. Chalks on paper, Tunis 2011

LAST LOVE-NOISE SOUND-NOTE

the pain was not only in having lost
her, her brown skin under
my pressing fingers:
I left that country in revolution,
In the medina howling middle-volt
of the al-Thawra, *Thawra
Horra Horra.* Back
to the world of gray spaces,
of loneliness,
bloodless gleaning
sanguine-loan
speeches,
women who lean in /
but not on balconies

Back.
to living under the regime
exile to cybernetic fortresses
whose installations and rule-gyres
send legitimate jurors
who deem
the moon
inadequate,
cruel deceiver, a demon
I etch on the pavilion
not to leave
a drawing,
but to break
through the shield they built *Anti-*
Against the sea

that saw how and with whom
the moon-canoe goddess Tanith
first conceived
the daughter Love,
as leaves of the milk-blooded tree, Frangipane
tendril-gathered around her legs
that emitted
 the waves

REMEMBERING TUNISIA

Until then it was not clear that life was worth living.
My heart is entangled,
in those crooked minarets,
in the makeshift tv antennas
with aluminum foil for reception,
in the blue-painted lattice-work in the shape
of the heart of a Berber queen of Carthage.
In the status symbol junk denoting
each and every home of good social standing,
among chalk fortress and seaside Cartha-ghettoes--
In Bizerte,
and in the black sunglasses
of the Islamist queens
wearing leopard-skin hijab--
In the spider-legged lies of military police
on Rue de la Liberté,
who messed with me
for being a Jewish tourist taking pictures
of the synagogue encased
in barbed wire, like my heart
was a synagogue encased in barbed
electrified razorwire,
until I kissed her
on the balcony where
in the morning the whispers
the husk of African birds towards the sun-
rise would outdo and deafen
cries of the muezzin hypocrites.

My heart's mainline, aorta
was entangled in her fists,
hands so small they seemed
belonging to a tiny idol,
she was a little goddess Tanith
made of richest clay,
my heart a broken red record
scratched by some gold shrapnel
in that clay,
from a hidden streamlet
of the Gulf of Tunis where the Bey
of Tunis
turned into a stag, un-seraphic
for spying on a bather.
my ridiculous heart entangled
in myths and legends--

Until then I had not yet stood convinced,
a Marxist fool,
that mythology = the basis of reality,
at its heart, without question--

the synagogue of my heart
did not need casing walls of stone
or barbed wire:
such crowns are *so christian.*
Where gray walls
once stood
now magpies bathed singing,
singing Vandals
near Carthage and Kasserine--
— Song of Solomon and Sheba,
song of songs,
love-song.

the time of mourning over, I did not

know life was worth living:

that one could eat
from the pomegranate
and not only dust or memories.

my heart was entangled, by the
aorta, its main wire.
but jasmine-panhandler urchin kid
cupid, came then with a wire-clipper,
mischievous little gardener.

''My heart fell entangled ''

drawing in diary, Medina of Tunis 2012

BE ARROGANT

be arrogant,
  be arrogant
    be arrogant
went the song
for inspiring bedouin-troubadour strength--
the last quatrain she translated--
its title was
'song without translation'
on the balcony near where a minaret slept,
under bay-of-Tunis pelican,
moon-warmed, it dozed off.
sounds of Berber cries from a wedding
groomtribe's false nouveau wannabe
riche, *post-dictature* having their party
at the Lablaby eatery downstairs
the invincible *lalu* cries of the women
striking at minaret,
awakened pelican song-arrows broke
from once-tattooed bellies.

She translated the songs of Oumaima Khalidi,
(Songs for awakening at night,
nour al Qamar)
inevitably, Fairouz,
the song texts by Darwish

in her broken English,
then I put Piazzolla, Violeta Parra
I pointed out her favorite words in Spanish, like
"mi paloma" my pigeon

(Despite all the monumental talk and the imperious chatter-chins in blind,
desperate Europe
the people vaccinated against jinn
with invective, virulent rivulets
in latex and deep streamlets of concern
about the Arab women,
the positions they find themselves in,
Vis a visa the Arab problem and the Arab potions
the Arab poisons and the precarious positions
of the Arabs vis a Visa the Europeans.

That din against the jinn,
against all born of the smouldering,
and not of the vapour--
followed by the infinite apologetic lecture
against the crimes of Delacroix,
and other alleged, wind-sick mass murderers.
That din, that din I was forced to hear
for five years--
But the only inequality between us
was in height: when we stood I had to bend
over her
like beaten up crescent from a molten minaret
to thank her for translation.

then morning, only brown stain
of the desert of brown honeyed earth and sugar
amassed into a bird,
sleeps on my skin,

between my bone-vest and the ceiling,
on my lung-chest, a stain
a dreaming
that is not to be faded with soap or water,
she is brown residue
of one
of four rivers in paradise,
no dams contain
no soap or water remove this
brown stain of deserts this
song breaks all sieves in hell.
The substance will go unnamed,
priced above
enriched uranium--

her earth is honeyed in the sandal prints,
her snores, exposed to air
turn into crumbs of sugar, scatter them
in the *jardin* garden of the *jemma* mosque,
owned by rich fat Qataris
who try to buy downpour, Tunis and Tanith,
the Tunis moon, mosque-garden
where we dumped the chameleons
from their tomato-tin captivity
impulsively purchased
from one-eyed poachers
on the way to Mehdia,
Irresponsible
of us to buy those animals at the roadside,
without proper knowledge to prepare
Berber witchcraft broth
called *lablaby.*
The resulting sorcery conducted a revenge,
against bad muezzin-singers
and their robotic sabbatical,
the cracked jukebox in the minaret,

its discovery a scandal,
the magic of our shaking bed set in motion--

Avenging so many interruptions
of our dawn's half-awakened work
of dreaming brows together--
Cautionary lullaby:
the poached chameleons in a tin we had bought
From a Badu at the roadside,
within a morning
devoured all the flies and vowels,
hovel-poor digested vowels
that don't belong there anyway,
in the arrogant lines stolen from prayers
that litter Semitic youths' love poems.

And no more flies touched her brown skin,
only six-legged kisses, 8 eyed scorpion of praise
and no more bees attacked
the honeyed earth of her sandalprints.

We kissed without mercy, first each other
then the earth and I acquired the colour
of her substance,
her name____)__,
is after the substance of a river that feeds
12 gardens of paradise distilled,
sipped by Muhammad and his winged mule,
it left them drunk:
prey in need of rehabilitation,
Dr Moses over the mobile phone
Spoke from his cadillac
prescribing 50 prayers, Daily.

SHE SAID TO ME

She said to me Be arrogant,
be arrogant my love, and believe me
Ours will outlive
the less childish love
they have spoken of in the pale
church down the street,
for centuries of lonelyness; decades un-
requited Slavic postcards.
her eyes and buttocks pointed to the ceiling,
we painted with irises :
the iris of truth and the loneliness of god's saints,
ikoned in the ceiling.
In the little church opposite,
the envious faces cooled, nun-frocked
dead planets in a wooden zodiac,
conspiring for centuries,
hoping to engineer a super love
that will outlive ours.

So be arrogant my love, be foolish
and selfish in love
entering into battle against automaton,
against the greater arrogance
of mechanical fool outlived by its own lifelessness

(VRAIMENT)

31

Prev. page: ''Press Conference, at the Awards Ceremony'' Drawing, black and white, (opposite ''She Said to Me'')

Next page:

Colour chalk on paper, drawing '' Young Woman sitting at the terrace of Café L'Universe, Tunis'' 2011

REPETITION

(all along, I had believed the swans bark,
having heard that from a Russian
cousin from the tundra, now lost in pail-dark.)

On the other side of a mountain, a black bird stood
on a wall without a house--

I returned on the highway to Tunis
where she landed again on my shoulder,
introduced herself with a chirp.

Her name the name for a substance
of a river in paradise

swan of Carthage Salambo.

FACTATUM FACTOTEM

In both Hebrew and Arabic,
the rivers in paradise
run fourfold of paths and odes,
have names that parents can give their newborns
in Hebrew
these more often go to boys (see, *Yuval*)
in Arabic, to girls. (see, *Kaouthar*)

this is a factatum, factotem
I mention this not merely
to make Political-electric discharge:
River is not ever the same sex or beau-anatomy depending on what the
moon conceals
what crescents cut,
or stars crest noteworthy.

INTERLUDE FROM BEFORE THE LOVER
Poems from first visit to Tunisia, 2011

Aeneas

Pity me, I am a banished half-Jewman
who carried a switchblade across
Mountain ranges, Negevs to Regueb
and through Marais in Paris--
(Paris, who is better
than deserter Aeneas,
but still your enemy,
Oh denimed Dido-woman of Tunis.)

And I have cut women's underwear
off stiff-shallow breathing, quiet torsos
I have nearly killed
without necessity:
Wasteful,
unlike Carthaginian economy;
of ways foreign
to the vast, joyous Necropolis--
and
plunged, subterranean Tunis.

Aeneas left Dido to scream and empty her lungs
of the last dream beside a destroyed,
graffitti'd fountain
until she disappeared,
leaving only:
fibrillations
in the seagrass blades.
Leaving only: pair of sainted sandals
that all bow to and kiss,
despite the odor.

She left also: a wreath of sunlight
when he prioritized over her to found
a glorious shantytown
ugly, cancerous
upon the seven hills

What a Roman creep,
What a son of a bitch I did not tell
I did not tell I did not
as we laughed and conspired by the *Ouah'ah*
by that dried up police state
smoking Tanith brand
and Camel Light
when these finished,
smoking the flowers and fireflies between our teeth
I did not admit
to Carthaginian queens
in the nightbar full of champagne-warmed
rebellion and cold fear
(political policemen dress pink)

My last name, Desimone is Neapolitan,
My grandfather nonino in Argentina,
was an exile,
he played saxophone wail of banishment
from home-rock,
and dishonor sans return ticket
his first name: Romulo

(A LIE ABOUT) ROMULO

In the '90s
they'd found
his lungs stranded
upon Caribbean sea-purslane —
their wings full of oil
perhaps he'd sought
the African island Djerba he had drowned
in his own whiskey
and his old man shit
full of grief,
maize-dotted Ursa Minor

and
a smudge of
cigarette-
 tar
 from a last kiss

Tunis-Marseilles Airport Transfer Gate, May 2011

My Condition – The identity of the elaborate ass walking on the treadmill, and lured (or so it would seem) by the bucket of horsefeed dangling in its snout, happens to be none other than the ass of Lucius Apuleyus, who wrote *The Golden Ass* – the novel from Carthage about a man undergoing the ill fortune of metamorphosis, transformed into a donkey for having blasphemed at an altar of official religion.

Flowers at Topheth in Tunis

All love is forbidden love all desire is forbidden desire Fight only to seize
your beloved your desire
put on no mauve or gray-striped
 business snake-suits
to argue with a state
for your love-dream in the congress-dome
rough amor bound,
and dumbed down into a bill.
Statecraft, legalisms crush the necks
 of love-dreams
Worse than the armless embrace of a snake
Legal tablets were made by a bedouin
only for saying No. Break the tablets, ignore the law,
break it effortlessly--

That which is wished for
cannot live, swim or love inside
a cage made of laws and lined
with newspaper folded crows
of bad news,
fearing smiling cupids who pour kero-
sene to put out fires in the heart.

I want all I love
to be made illegal, criminal
so I can love these things and beings more
with bravadoes that make love unquestionable
such as courage, secrecy
fearless,
clandestine night of sensuality-athletes in amor,
naked, outrunning the night-mosques

of pimps who hate buddleida
and sisters of Noamen,
and all Syriac red flowers

Sidi Bouzid, Tunisia March 25, 2012
first published in The Brown Critique, New Delhi

Etude d'épreuve argentique, playing upon Landrock's picture from the Tunis brothel 1903
Drawing on paper

GOODBYE TUNIS

Goodbye opal-shard-dotted
 fair underarm I once kissed,

of Carthaginean Queens
The smell of glowing jasmine green fig
vermilion mouths of conspirators
smoking in Avenue Habib Bourguiba

Obsidian hair of Arrwa and Malek
greasy in palm (greasy and black
 but more like Elysium than fairest, blondest wheat)

during a demonstration
the Palm trees parted like women for our procession
We were no caravan of despair:

These grains of quartz
wander the ramparts
of my singing lungs,
lamppost of my spine;
porticoes of my Semitic nostrils,
like rainflies marooned after mercy,
dying and resurrecting again,
sub-Carthage moon-canoe
followed by Dido's Patron, Venus
Latin for Aphrodite
who Arabs once adored at Jerasch Maddabah
at Kabah, over Mecca.
Venus, Aphrodite/ Morning star:
This is why at 4 AM,
before the sun,
they still salute "Morning of her Light,

Morning of She with Flowers and Jasmine!"

(Marseilles Airport Transfer Gate, May 2011)

prev.: drawing ''Raha – Liberator, the /Free'' ''The Persian Raha, freedom fighter as the Kahina, the Berber liberator Queen. 2011

KANTHUS REVOLUTIONARY

Left side, drawing: Portrait of an Activist Casbah-Watcher, made upon Request, India ink 2011 Fi Casbah

TUNISIAN WOMEN ACTIVISTS[2]

Dido never really died
Di- do
and
All you
Queens of Carthage:
should the secret police
in their pink striped suits,
touch one obsidian hair:
I will slit their throats,
I will sink their little motor
-boats

All those secret cops,
work for the great Stellar pimp
dressed in pinstripe plainclothes,
with a vulgar tricolour French flag-pin,
the wannabe.

Yeah, those tranquil policemen
work for the Supreme Pimp--

I will shoot them
till they walk with a limp,
should they dare curse-breathe or bugger
one obsidian hair.
Beware, beware,
should they touch 1 singular
obsidian hair

Didaun, unruly Dido
Never truly died
on this or that day B.C
This was Didaun's most singular Lie,
sung from reddest, genuine Pulse that orbed.
Once she's cobbled
her Pulse back together,
the segments of disheveled red tulip bulb,
she barely needs me,
To drown her enemies
She doesn't depend
only on me,
to tighten the pink scarf
of her enemy--
but it's the gesture that resonates.

Birds over Mainframes 1

the birds fall like *Sidi*-saints

who delved into the earth of Sidi
Bouzid, Sidi Bousaeed and died
there, became a *Oua'hah* shrine there--

small myth: their fine bones
are keys to the enclosures of kings,
the immortal worms that tunneled
the corpses of these birds
immediately upon being seen,
overpower the seer to swallow them:
and he will carry them in his stomach
where they harvest vineyards of suffering
that spring like a revolutionary speech
from his mouth,
and the misery
can only be destroyed when immersed
in the water of one
of the four
rivers in paradise, Koranic *firdaus*--
this is the most violence,
that medieval Islamic Ornithology
of Ibn Khaldoun and the Sidi doctors
proved capable of.

BIRDS OVER MAINFRAMES 2

If we still knew how to train birds
to send and bring the letters, warrants,
 papyri to fear or anticipate,
declarations and refusals of love, subpoenas—
then we wouldn't ever need to mainframe
Only to leave little indentures
and stone bowls full of water,
some seeds and *Attarsheya* flowers
for the birds,
like what Arabs leave by their mother's graves
in cemeteries of dry dirt under sun
And every third window
would be busy
with birds coming and going,

No one would squabble over computers
virtual telegrams
all of us transistor-mechanics on flat bureaus,
reading one another's morse code
faceless blank books

Instead of a send-lever
we would dispatch the message
by kissing the bird on its head,
read throat, thumb on picking beak,
then throw it at sky's cloud-brains
that never fall or cease dreaming

and our messages would not
crash or fall to die in the wingspan
of its own dirt-hugged shadow

Effort is necessary to pick the fastest bird,
the prettiest,
or the most gray,
depending on the nature of the message
and the beauty of the recipient:
orange black Troupial, who sings sweetly,
the Caribbean Chuchubi, gray and hoarse
announces death by blue-tailed grape-thief lizard
African Swallow: faster than mercury
the merchant
of financial underworlds,
he holds the legal codes
of Cupid speeding through treetops
where violets grow over the wet cemeteries
and the hammocks of passion's recipients.

Poem on the Theory of the why and how/ and the not now of the Revolux

Revolutions can only happen in paradises
that are un-self -aware,
Argentina before the coup—
Legend: young ladies stooped
to talk to a fellow reading
a book by that skew-eyed le grande frog Sartre
or to read one by that saint Genet, thieving fag.
Skirts still long and black,
for Argentine autumn they had just
re-discovered jazz,
there was no cocaine
and the name Paco, for sons
and not yet given to crack cocaine,
poor ate the bread of wicked in hovels,
dreamed of not working, of revolution:
the poor, at times, read novels
and contacted los amigos, the other poor
las almas not *los amos*
("the spirits")   ("the masters")

they stood at the scaffolded top of the concert hall
named " Paradiso, "
a grandiose skull unbenched in that baroque,
misshapen deaf pearl flooded with sound,
the Teatro romantic dreams and drumroll,

revolutionary étude* on piano
(by Chopin not Perón*)
The illiterate can read what is sung,
of what is sung, the illiterate can read novels:
novels undreamed of
by the erudite deaf of letters.

A country must be tender and naïve,
where illusions are flowers competed over
by populace without
desire for infini- uni- screen-television,
where sexual liberation is a song of rebellion
that does not down-load,
merely to free the overload
to welcome the new leaden.

revolutions are in countries
where people are sweet,
where even the hypocrisy is sweet--
like Tunisia.

Whereas revolutions in high-modern,
post-post intellectual society
would be considered full of kitsch,
then condemned
to the recycle-bin.

revolutions don't happen after a second series
of administrated massacres,
revolutions are of people
who remained sweet ,
and childish, like fresh-plucked tamarinds,
stolen, illegal treat,
collective and lonely
dancing Samson Tender-feet.

LETTER SHE ASKED NEVER TO PUBLISH

Thank you, Ouafa Hind for the photographs
depicting me as the swimmer-Maritime monarch,
Poseidon or one possessed by him
in the art of mimicking the wave.
Maybe I behaved more like a cycloptic ogre,
Son of Poseidon, in my selfish depression
Yesterday when we woke.
never been so happy as during days with you/
Foolish of me to have believed
that I know what lovers were,
or what it meant to make
the hoop of love/
Hope I am able to show,
how you look in my one eye

I know Poseidon had a daughter called Ouafa, ___
She brought you to me
like a six-legged starfish in the claw of an African bird
of Carthage Salambo,
that in turn slept on my shoulder
I knew I must have done a thing right
I wish you could see
the Ouafa I see
Your pictures say so much
Sorry if I ever let cynicism
slip into my single eye that
normally views reality more focused,
strong cyclops,
more eye-magnet-force
than the two-eyed,

when I said Iloveyou, *Ana b'habik*
you did not answer with words,
certainly not to an ogre who knows no Arabic.

Come, my honeyed earth,
to keep the river from the land
of the dead
from entering
through the floor
of cedarwood to make walls
that still let in
kind scarab beetle,
form enclosures of shade,
for gardens of the lovers waiting
to see apricots break into flower
and birds into song upon eating tastira
and lablaby.

Our art is about us:
it is from who and what
we are, it saves us and loves we who serve it,
with lilies crushed in our mouths
of faith and violence walking on knees slid
from Carthage or Golgotha.

and lovers who are artists
can also save their love with their art, and serving it.
though it takes more than just making art
to save lovers, and I must remind myself of this,
to be more "earth to earth" as you, in Arabic say.

PERSEUS

Perseus threw

    away

        the Gorgon-head.

In its place, head of a girl: dark-eyed,

named "White Antelope" in Arabic nascent from neck,
(consonants born, then pronounced
in a throat burdened, unburied.)

Like a leaf that healed
noiselessly, she stood there
in impermanent town of white graves: Mehdia--

Birds drown out the noise,
carry in the candle of day,
gathered
like sea-grape pollen,
from the Mehdia sea
in big claws.

The fruits hung upside down, like genitalia,
parted,
so they could see us from their hideouts
in the date palm trees,
leaves like skirts

offered to naked women

in heaven of secret bodies

IN EUROPE THE FIGS ARE POISONED

The figs are poisoned in europe Catullus won
he wiped out the crows from the fig trees saying they look like Indians,
crows berbers monkeys.
He was a master of oratory rhetoric, euphemistic

Refined by him, the crowd made loans
to Scipius Africanus,
who ate a scorpion,
at the seaside banquet
out of greed ate scorpion--
because he mistook it
for a lobster.
The cook, an African, fed it to Scipius.

The figs are all poisoned in europe,
the europeans watch the revolution projected
on a purplish skin of a resinous immense eggplant
on a fig
they can't tell the two apart,
 scions of Catullus' wealth
And they applaud:
it is a flowered gladiatorial match
they want to see the Arabs against Arabness
conflict foreign to the shamed Roman circuses
of Sidi Bousaeed,
where an Arab knelt to Aphrodite,
just once, then renamed her

the landless in Tunisia are in love with flowers
The europeans want the flowers without leaves,

All the tragedies of recent history bear relation to this

Note for orthographical zealots: Europa, the Persian once abducted by the Olympian bull no longer wants it named after her, therefore the little ''e'' un-capitalised.

REVOLUTION OF THE ARCHAIC

My poems are irrational,
dark unconscious phantom literature,
Bacchic violent, torture chamber,
Mantuan apothecary
revolution of the archaic
The way the enemy seeds for oil and erases the archaic
I seed for the wine
and erase the post-modern
What do you do about it
I will never be a sober augur,
calm in wisdom poems, like Vallejo like Cesar

But I gave up the search for the cure at a young age,
I gave up a boyhood delinquent holygrail quest
 to cure grandiloquence
And I want to know
who hid Madness,
 and said it is Arabness

and I went to retrieve a Crown
ever since I gave up the search
 for a cure for the cathartic.

World without Misery

All my life and dawn of youth I hated Buddhist hypocrites, under their big
feathered polyurethane turbans
smiling positivistic
but I would not disbelieve that Life is Suffering
that all Life equals Suffering

I tried to build a compromise
around this favorite concept, clay key to the gates of dawn, where ogre
beggars
stretch their yellowed arm from great fork crutch for coins that will not
suffice
to pay off debts
to the eternal bill-collectors
to ferry-man who transports the dead shades across the long rivers of
contempt they still shove the coins under their eyelids,
desperate, they are out of eyelashes

Painting with etymology:
in Latin, the word for 'Passion'
 is the same as for 'Suffering,'
Passus
Yes--
bite into the Passionfruit--
face pinches in pain,
sweet, you see, Suffering is also
Passion, and worthwhile:
I argued this.
even though I hated Catholics
and Jesuits Christians as well
who smiled positivo-severe
under their Byzantine turbans,

Lotus-eaters hiding
mineral spoils in their hats,
wealth of stolen menorah gulped,
hidden in guts of Apology-fish
candelabrum-branch-lit bankruptcies.

Vain under their turbans,
tweezed eyelashes immune to REM-twitch
and catching no dust of dreams
of burning cypresses.)

But I was a revolutionary:
"For there is Suffering, you see,
and then there is Misery,
and a difference between the two.
"Suffering is passion and we cannot
have a world without fish-bites
that take our feet, cannot ever
defeat it, it is natural, kinetic
of the burden of our freedom in our lungs

"but misery is artificial, constructed.

"See the difference between the coca
plant sacred to sun-dirtied Indians,
and cocaine white powder
of laboratory processes,
capital-money
of the tall great snivelers.

"Misery of the favelas
of the children of starving fools.
"Establish that this alone we can abolish:
Misery,
Must be abolished!

"But Suffering--
Suffering is here to stay,
the everyday Realists
and fantasists at once!
"For the sight of misery numbs us,
thin lions struggle
over crumbs--
that is not suffering,
that prevents passion:
like cocaine,
or condom complications
prevent passion between
those who saw each other's
fluttering eyes
in the forest and forgot
they had minds,
and were superior
to birds, dragons,
barbarians and other animals
who do that beastly deed
called love."

"They had drunk of the water kept
by a grave, for the birds who brought pollen
to the earth of dead
and were punished in their neurons.

"Utopia
is a world of suffering without misery:
we learned,
through suffering, the intelligence:
Avoid Miseria, vanity
well-splicing the seeds of nowheres,
the burns made by rational fantasy.

Out, fear!
"But one cannot go
without suffering,
the bird who did not want
to lift himself
from the acacia he loved,
to return to Africa in time
to clude the winter god tribes' attack.

"From his chest, fused to a tree, refusing disembark
therefrom spring the sinful roots of our world,
oppression.
I am not shamed by the
ever-presence of suffering,
in my adrenaline dreams
of Inhibitionist sexuality--"

In my science
I thought myself clever, original--
tested the theory,
rolling a wheel
setting off lights:
Simulacrum from the glass
in the laboratory
of my demagoguery of ingenious loneliness,
the first who noticed the distinction:
Science means to cut, to split apart: scissor.

But now I was with her in the car on the high-
way, past Binzarrat,
across the fields of wild vineyards.
Lightning overhead might make the best wine
of these fields,
the lighting presses the grapes:
like bare feet of Egyptian nuns

upon grapes.
The cows look like how they appear
in the pictures from ancient Egypt,
holding the setting sun
between their horns, (true *Thawra*)
carrying the purpled azure
our bodies full of rosé and

it has changed my mind-helmet,

Life was not this,
Life is the end-island
where suffering does not reach

and all the buddhists, the Lotus-eaters
and Christians
with their passive-aggression preach
of *Passus*
under their turbans,
under their grand tabula rasas,
are dead as dead cats with glassed stomachs
to be tossed in the sunlit dirt streets
of our island enclosure,

where laughter is fragrant as meats
and rose pours the red wine
into our glasses
containing the sun of first kiss
at the gates of dawn

(the small ranch had calves,
we hid from the children,
behind the golden wall of calf-butts,
smelling of such)

somewhere between
Sidi Bousaeed and
Sidi Bouzid.

DECEPTION /Tunisienne

I had believed her,
when possessed in the restaurant,
shadows from the wine,
against white and blue cloth, those
colours of saturn
turn wine spilled from the drunken
mouth of Tanith,
deity of moon-canoe .
The thin waiter smoked outside, he did not
see the spectacle of possession,
his shadow elongated,
like a wheat plant growing
quietly rising by moonlight,
his shadow then scattered like oil
over a beach,
where by day the martyred
love-children of Carthage dreamt in flotsam
hoping the one god will heart-break again,
like a pomegranate into a manyness
of Semite gods,
rupture symbiosis of the seeming one-god,
fill the goblets, raise cups and invisible guns--
shout, declare "Dionysos was a Tunisian--
Dionysos, the first Tunisian!"

the waiter shouted and in a *Thawra* threw
his hourly cigarette rolled of dark cold sea-winds.
A naked goddess Tanith stood

in the long window,
lit the dark brown tamarind full lips
across the table, after we drained
our commanded 10th glass
of wine.
The crystal cups somehow permanently full,
vivid, we could not *vide*-empty them,
trying with our mouths,
insipid struggle, futility.
The waiter insisted--with a grimace,
a grudge--
that Dionysos is a Tunisian,
as he cleared the table
of the children's crumbs,
the fish scales and the cooked sandals
rechristened as trout, *a la carte*
the cooked toy minaret
named swordfish,
it was good
as godless, crescent made
filet in skillet--
smiling knees carried us to the car,
and kept the keys during our turpitude,
examined and burnt by the moon.
The moon is Tannith's
Body, not her Brain

Then Chekov said

Then, Chekov said
*"Men deprived of the company of women
become stupid,
women, deprived of the company of men, pine"*
I do not know from which portal
of the moon the desert
descended from upon these fortresses
Wherefrom the omen, pale guardian
who stood between me and every
woman and Beloved like an ancient boxer of Smyrna
Bronze ancient Aztec, Sumerian,
Akkadian boxer

I am a poet of the order
of murderers gone conscientious,
who with able footwork
avoided the patron god and goddess
of the orders of thieves
in a match for iron life upon the water,
my nose grew big and round and shiny red
as I shouted like a hard head,
needing an axe from within
my brow of dreams dormant,
I did not sleep,
yet my wakefulness
was not that of the lover,
and in the Southern islands
and in the thaw,
it was autumn,
On the day after New Year's,
In the tropical island of my birth

it was already autumn,
the aloes and cacti unstirred,
the yellow houses with a red light,
already ash Wednesday
of the ash-worshippers
sharp song-canoes came out doorways
 of clay churches I knew better than to enter

Poem Spectavorticle:
Love poem for a non-existing woman.

"Spectacle exerts very great powers of attraction on the soul." Lodovico
Castelvetro Cavorting scream
throw my arms up like a brigand my barbarie is a joke
hologram impersonation
dances for sex, for straw dogs of forgiveness
to be thrown again unto the electric flame desire animate hysteria

Introverted I am,
as the Etruscan who sits at stylite's foot

My secret as a boy of eight: I had wanted
to kiss the Sphinx on her lips and breasts of cinnamon and lift her tiger-tail.

Introverted I am,
but if you are my love
then I will make a Spectacle for you and a Spectacle out of you.

bushels of apricots
whose weight you did not know you carried fall from your arms and pants to
the concrete *thud, thud*

your eyes darken

the pedestrians adjust their glasses, lenses,
hike up their collars and march away on indignant feet in 300 euro
newspaper shoes
we remain barefoot, but it is less cold.

Goodbye To One Named After the Residue of 1 of 4 Rivers in Paradise.

The vase is full of death
The water in the vase is full of death

The abandoned house
I found on the arid winter road, broke in--
broke brass doorhandles clunked
and I filled it proudly,
until luminescent with 100 flower brushes
from the river-bay:
tall flowers I set for her have died.

They litter the walkways
where no more dancing of villagers
has occurred, shaking the hemlock groves.
No unbosoming about her
to friends in a thousand beers,
no lovers or commiserators,
no brother-losers--
not in any phase of orbs.

The vases that I dug up, lit up,
cleaned, now stand
full of death well-balanced the house,
my world has vanished from this garden-ghetto,
whose light came from another world.
she no longer waits
and I no longer wait for her.

"En el Norte de Formosa, son menos atrevidos" or "Tucumán Tunisia Blues" drawing

LETTER OF WANTS

I want to talk to you,
    from time
        to
       time.
Tragedies can be unmade,
and making new ones is unnecessary.
I want to be able to talk to you
without hesitation and resentment and fear.
Do not seal away
our contact in a jar,
in the dry earth
for the night of awaiting nightboats.
Do not seal away
every last vestige
of a season's weak memory,
of the apparition of walking down
a street of white graves
when there was something worthwhile,

There is nothing to fear from me:
nothing is far,
my face was on fire,

my heart was a hive of winged
insects fallen from a cedar in a fire
that the sea has cancelled,
I go to the sea
who is a physician, and lives near Cordoba,
Granada, Sidi Bousaid, Athens
and all the places

I have not yet been to*   (* *Bintoon*بنت *"girl"*)

but I can look up the address,
and he will treat me like a fire,
with free
and gratis health insurance.

I, physician, will not allow
your small hands
to seal off our remembering
in a special wall, special tomb
underneath layers of earth farmed dead dry,
where the dead sleep,
waiting for a winged motorboat,
iding from the jackals (they
are known grave-eaters)

I want
to speak to you again,
and that our voices are not dead in each other's souls

WHITE ANTELOPE

This time I fall
and am surprised,
it is no acted fall like the ones I was good at.
The White Antelope has lain
 next to me, knocked out from my blue and red
vital organs—
it lies there, sable-white and blinking, wounded.
I fear I
have tunneled out the best in me.
It blinks and I comfort it,
Kiss its black lips,
feed it prayers.
I fight the fly's
descent on us,

How did it get in here
into the airtight bookroom?

It had lived in these Italian catacombs,
between liver and kidney and lung,
and rotting all this time,
or I rotted it. I could not give it
as a gift. As a dowry for womb-right
buying the first nocturne.
It stayed here, treated as if
Worthless as my isolated life,

Obsolete as I am, repressed, censored
Error-writer. I cradle it,
try to whisper it back to life

Vortices of sights that are neither dreams
Nor shadows: shadows are what the sun extends
From its maniacal mansion-heart
Of concentric slums
Shadows are its truth.
Without shadows the splendour-sun
would be helpless as the shadows amputated,
without the sun,
as woman of fair or ill repute
lacking parasol of a dainty man
to bring her topaz songbird,
or the lunar salt won
as man sans woman (infernal bore)
as island sans import,
songless bird, perched on petrol, or gun
as woman without flattering comparisons to
this or that sun, this or that moon of Jupiter,
this or that Jerusalem
of iron or gold,
this bird or
that gazelle.

POEM OF ENDINGS FOUND IN GOOGLE SEARCH

No longer a resident of your skin,
having lost all official permits
in the vomit stream of papers that self-cremate
like good citizens, and mosque-villains
in the vanilla nothing-nada-ness screens
of the great Karmic chains of emails,
that self-edit by way
of the window-wipers equipping
their flying, foreign, future cars:
the modern vipers
that once clung to the winged by the ankles,
Pretending to be winged serpents, fangs spreading
their fuel, and that way, like oil emirs they
parasitically rode the sky-ramps.
I have a stamp in the estranged
and vanished republic of you, and in
our stratospheric fortress of fear and love
in the old fashioned way letters
in vanilla-creme scented envelopes seamed
with a bit of gunpowder for a New Year
that never came,
Scurrilous my fingers enter your name, Enshrined
in the Search Engine, like playing
octave on a broken clarinet
and it is
steam-operated, the onyx steam darkens my eyes
like Octo-ink, alternating from
good clean old coal. See the net.

You are famous. I, unknown perhaps the price paid
for not wearing a turtleneck, a smock of trainers and athletes
or perhaps, for being the only
poet outspoken in his support for nuclear energy.
With your name in the Latin spelling
knitted into the Fortress of Search Engine, I pull an effortless lever and I know
what has become of you. I am
No longer a resident of your skin,
You are famous.
But no matter how many triggers I pull
with finger, with tongue, with investments and accouterment
intestines like the first musical bow-ancestor
of all the instruments, pens I wrote in like fire-penises
I used to chronicle my auto-bestiary
I cannot find what became of me.
I search I cannot unearth
what became of me.
The ramps of Dr Schmidt's Rx medicine Google
tell me my location, "Try refresh page"
recommends technician in chat. Garage of blanks
But the page grows arthritic, in impatience,
sick like my grammar
(in this foreign language
I calligraph sabotage in,)
and forgets the aliastic name it was told to tell Motoh,
the visiting angel of death, collector
of dead butterflies for sacrifice
Rationed
in the traditional mortuary
way of Aztecs
for as Coltrane whistled "I'm old fashioned"
over his brassy lo-tech—

TUCUMÁN-TUNISIA BLUES

I cleared the room of the babel
of cheap dead papers, peeled off the walls
that rustled as I had tried to sleep,
rolled them and set to soak in a bucket
out with all old mildewed death
that kept me mired
in Buenos Aires when I should have been
at the Iguazu, watering the ruins
left by Jesuits and Guaranis.

On the window-ledge, my plants:
the aloe thrived, fool's crown,
long spiney tendrils, strong as an octopus
crawling without thirst--
jasmine has been stolen,
from the balcony
by the blackhaired daughter
of the opinionated butcher from Tucuman.
The purple violet has died,
left only a black earth circle
the *na'anna* plant dead,
left only clod
of red earth
upon which I pick up 2 halves
of a broken scarab beetle,
and my mouth rebels
against my brain,
and the soul that orbs it--
muttering something about how

my Arab girl
across the ocean in Tunisia,
no longer thinks of me,
no longer waiting,
no longer

POEM MORPHO / VOYAGES OF AN ERRANT NARCISSUS

In the Caribbean island,
I was the unsmiling Russian boy--
Immigrated to Northern Europe,
into a white African:
logically, I went to Tunisia
to locate the revolution presumed farcical,
but there, my head turned blond,
roots in Normans,
who fertilized my ancestresses
in their fortresses upon the sea-grass
and bones of Jews and Sicilians, Africans--

the chromatosis helped,
at least I found
brown love at last, to Arab music,
naked poetry, nour-al-kamra'aaa

Inexplicably I was always hated in Amsterdam /
Inexplicably was always drawn to where I could be hated.

pristine streets and lampposts
kissed my roaring, shoe-pricked spine
with an ancient memory,
that was not the body's Shekinah
 of primitive Jewish medicine.

I cursed the goyim unborn,
my hair and eyes turned black
my nose awful strong,
long, crooked, a crook, a hook,
catching fat-bottomed mermaids--

Punished for plucking a last
colonised tulip
with my crazy gnashing moonlit
hungerface: folkloric mask of
indigenous Babi Yar/Treblinkan snake-child
slithering on his abdomen,

the hoarded moon flower
Tulip they stole from Turkman
(they tricked him, promising
travel-and love insurance):
I
ate it

Those Who Dwell Amongst the Rocks
An Extremely Brief History of the Tunisian Revolution[1]

Tunisia has received honourable mention in the international press as one of the few ''success stories'' of the Arab spring. Yet it seems the major conflict of interest that has divided Tunisia, played out between the Western and Gulf Arabian interests that hoped to co-opt the Arab Spring revolutions on one side, and the actual intentions, dreams and immense optimism of the Tunisian people—and of the young in particular. The more cynical of Western critics of the ''Arab spring'' see only the disappointments resulting from a Western push for regime change in the Middle Eastern and North African region. French and the American military interventions, alongside the interests of European allies and investors, all sought to usher in a new order with a more deregulated economy, open entirely to the market and to foreign investment, regardless of the opinions of the Arab protesters as to what they deemed good for them. Dictators like Libyan Muamar Ghaddaffi, Iraq's Saddam Hussein and Syria's Assad had presented their regimes as protective welfare states that nurtured their grateful citizenry. The revived Islamist parties in the region showed they mostly favoured de-regulation of the old state apparatus, despite the Islamist guerrillas having once enjoyed much support from the poor and the exploited. The poor, once made more

---

[1] This essay first appeared in the political magazine *CounterPunch* in 2015.

vulnerable by the eradication of the secular state, would in turn rely on the Mosque as a place of social assembly and support: thusly the Islamists justified their gamble with market-fundamentalism married, chimerically, to Islamic fundamentalism.

But for many protesters there was much more at stake: namely, the freedom to speak one's mind about their countries' state of affairs, and to democratically choose governments without the police State's threats of censorship, torture or disappearance. Perhaps the optimism of their post-authoritarian political vision prevented many of these youthful movements from noticing the Trojan horse of foreign interests vying for power, stationed at their city gates from Carthage to Damascus.

News of Tunisia's revolts, ousting the Benali regime in 2010, was immediately followed by a tumultuous period of post-dictatorship and unrest: that which is universally referred to as "transition." Forces of popular rage had involved many groups in Tunisian society, now wielded ecstatically together in uprising. Most important among these, were the passionate and often well-educated youth of the working and middle classes, often faced with chronic unemployment, unable to emigrate easily to Europe, and beset by the claustrophobia of living in a small police state led by the Benali family and their "Mauve party' of decadent authoritarianism. The crowds vying to usurp back their stolen power included supporters of workers' unions, political parties of the Left and of the religious Right, counting participants of all ages.

Their assemblies were at times a chaotic pandemic, despite the organizational efforts by clandestine and forbidden political parties that had lived as underground networks even before Benali's coup replaced the previous dictator Habib Bourghuiba. (the most legendary example is the leftist Workers' Party leader Hamma Hammami, who at times had lived hidden in sewers and basements until he emerged to lead the communist insurgency in 2010. Unsurprising then, that Hemma Hammami's life and loves became the stuff of popular legend among Tunisian high-school students of the generation born under the fearsome Benali.) A change in the geopolitical and imperial sphere suggested there would not be any more cold-war Western support for Benali's regime (once a much-favoured client state for both France and the United States' foreign policy)—allowing the ragtag social movements to commit the first popular overthrow of a dictator in the 21st century Arab world.

After the ousting of Zine el-Abidine Benali, there reigned a general, euphoric chaos in the crowds. Any Tunisian taking part in a crowd was suddenly an activist, self-declared, all constantly tested the limits of this mysterious concept of freedom they had heard so much about. The crowds stood outside of the major institutes of power, such as the Supreme Court or the "Casbah" —where they awaited the rulings by judges of former political prisoners and the policemen who had offended their rights. They chanted the lines from the poet Abu-Qasem El Chebbi which include the verse "Those who do not wish to climb the mountain, shall dwell amongst the rocks" Chebbi was a poet who, like the patriot-poets of many countries under domination during the era was committed to the quest for national independence. (Adam Miciewicz, poet and liberator of Poland, or Jose Martí, poet and rebel-leader for the cause of Cuban Independence, come to mind as possible comparisons to Chebbi).

Chebbi formed part of the Tunisian DesTour party in the early 20th century and even fought as a guerrilla. His poem became an anthem of all the Arab uprisings that broke loose in 2010-2011. The militant verse, in places, sounds oddly Protestant though romantic: those who are indolent in the struggle for liberty, those who will not climb the mountain can do as they please, but are warned they will be abandoned to live amongst the rocks (not necessarily like those who inhabit rock-dwellings in the extreme South of the country, in Tataouine overlooking the Sahara.)

During the most recent revolts, fire-lit lines from Chebbi competed amongst the crowds with chanted prayers of the Quran. Quranic quotes about resilience were mouthed by those supporting the Muslim Brotherhood and related movements, distant from the left and yet as relevant in the steps towards overthrowing Benali, the surprised ruler who fled to Saudi Arabia. Despite his notoriety, hated by the Muslim Brotherhood as a secular oppressor, Benali was welcomed to live out his exile in Saudi Arabia, the main supporter of the ISIL/Daesh militias today, which include many Tunisians, North Africans and European children of North African immigrants among their ranks.

Tunisia's revolts of 2010 claimed the lives of between 300 and 340, killed by the military and snipers—these mostly unarmed protestors, whether or not they were religious qualified as shaheedeen, martyrs. When I travelled the Central and Southern provinces, young men who participated in a Tunisian ''Festival de la Revolution'' cultural festival showed me the town of Regueb. Reguebians told me what may have been a myth of the revolution: that Benali's gendarmerie and snipers had chased youths they knew, who were ruthlessly burnt alive while hiding in mosques that were firebombed by the army. If true, then such a desperate tactic pronounced the end of any obedience to the RCD (Constitutional Democratic Rally, the single party of Benali and his predecessor Bourghuiba) Now in 2015, one of the scandals affecting Tunisian society is the high rate of recruits to ISIS/Daesh who came from these regions. It is a disheartening national trauma for the Tunisians, who would have wanted to express solidarity with the Syrians and Iraqis. (Many youths in the South-Central region who were part of the Islamist groups and who witnessed the Syrian tragedy on television and through the internet—simplified as another secular oppressor, Assad, former ally of Benali, brutally cracking down on his own people—convinced them to join Libyan, Algerian and European Islamists in the self-righteousness of armed missions, supported then by Al Qaeda and by none other than US Secretary of State John Kerry to attempt a violent overthrow of Bashar al-Assad.)

Transition's Carnival and Foes

During the Tunisian 2011-2013 period of transition, the crowds and political parties were pitted against counterinsurgency, consisting of the many intricate structures of political police and the remnants of the Benali regime. The religious right wing, the Ennahda or "Dawn" party won the first elections by a landslide, out of the more than 70 political parties that had suddenly risen into existence during the period of tumult during and after the revolt. Ennahda had strong roots in the rural Centre and South of the country, where many of the poor and exploited agricultural labourers lived. Ennahda, whose party logo is a hawk in flight, channelled the historical divisions and resentments of the South against the North: most of the soldiers who fought the French in the war of independence were conscripted by Habib Bourghuiba from the countries' rural centre and south; many pro-Bourghuiba families in the North speak better French than their Arabic and have lived in a historical delusion about independence, believing that independence was handed-over in a non-violent and bureaucratic pact of peace-making by the French, as a bloodless concession to Bourghuiba. Eventually, such cognitive dissonance worsened between the children of the resistance fighters and the "Carthagineans" of the more affluent port-cities by the sea. Many among the elites sincerely believed no such anti-colonial war had taken place in an African former French colony, perhaps a reassuring thought given the extent of French culture they have come to identify with, regardless of how French xenophobia might disagree or frown upon the North Africans' sentimentality.

Purification

Within the transitional or "provisional inter-rim government" were former officials of the Mauve-party, Benali's loyals: a scandalous state of affairs led to calls for what was called "épurations"in French, purifications or East-European-style 'lustration'-campaigns and trials to purge the old-regime elements from all institutions except for the police (where it would have proven impossible to "purify"). Such campaigns were called for by young politicians, often of those families most affected by the police and surveillance state with its practices of psychological and physical torture. Many even called for a death penalty—yet these remained at sentimental wishes, rage sublimated in Facebook democracy. The former "party families," those people who wore the violet/mauve colour because it was Benali's favourite, quickly switched their political allegiances either to the Islamist party or, less opportunistically to the Nidaa Tounes neoliberal centre-right party. This part of Tunisian society is often caricatured by the widely-beloved underground cartoonist Zed, in his popular series 'Debat-Tunisie' as the "Ben Simpsons": petit-bourgeois dwellers of the "posh" neighborhoods such as La Marsa and Carthage in Tunis, who created an American-style consumer way of life. The very influential and real "Ben Simpsons" group are lampooned in the comic strip as being chameleonic and opportunistic, wearing either mauve or hijab (or a mauve hijab) if it caters to the political whims of the day; suddenly the Ben Simpsons go Islamist and pray to the wrong direction; elsewhere they congregate around a giant crate of the Tunisian *Celtia*-brand of local beer, thinking it is Mecca.

Ben Simpsons' always opportune world has generally been a happy petit-bourgeois affair, despite the many Tunisians who were imprisoned or murdered by the political police, Zed's hilarious and dirty pictures are an art form, and luckily gaining more recognition. The cartoonist expressed his being appalled at the murders of the Charlie Hebdo cartoonists (a killing spree that was also followed by the supermarket attack, during which at least one Tunisian was killed.)

Between Two "Third Ways"

When the new cannot emerge and the old cannot die, then we are living in the time of monsters
–Antonio Gramsci

The two largest parties in Tunisia are both variations of "Third Way" rhetoric: post-political parlances, often expressed in moralistic and slightly utopian terms, seeking out the "third way" alternative route between capitalism and Soviet era socialism. On the right, the Islamists—led by Rached Ghannouchi and other former political prisoners—and in the "extreme centre," Nidaa Tounes, party of technocrats, post-politics and neoliberal solutions, is led by current president Essebsi, a former official of Tunisia's first, founding dictatorship. Between the religious and secularist "Third Way" parties, there seemed to be one rising party that achieved a stunning popular upswing during the years of 2013, only to be met with repression: the Tunisian left, politically embodied in the unions and in the "Movement of Democrats and Patriots" the Red Party whose daring spokesmen Chokri Belaid and Mohamed Brahmi would soon be assassinated.

Shortly after entering office in October 2011, Ennahda began to disappoint the labourers in the South, who were promised workers' rights and higher wages; but were instead punished with the illegalization and dissolution of the unions (a betrayal similar to Erdogan's sudden turn against the striking miners in Turkey.)

As political Islam and the once-romanticized Muslim Brotherhood party lost the broken heart of its supporters, the radical left grew in regions like

Sidi Bouzid, where descendants of Touareg nomads lived in the conditions of sweltering poverty that first made the revolts explode with Mohammed Bouazzizzi's public self-incineration. Much of Ennahda's opposition demanded that Ennahda and its leaders take measures against the Salafi extremists who were wreaking havoc in Tunisia. Ennahda was the Muslim party which promoted itself as moderate and whose politicians, many of them former political prisoners, compared themselves to European Christian-Democrats, despite their being a variation of moderate and puritan-extremist believers within the party. (Erdogan, who up until recently enjoyed a more positive image as a ''lenient'' religionist, was also a model for the Tunisian Islamists.) Salafists, mostly gangs of young bearded men who were formerly social outcasts and ridiculed as losers in Tunisian society, began to vandalize traditional Sufi and Berber graves and to attack artists and art galleries, such as the attack on the Printemps des Arts festival exhibition that resulted in a fire in 2012 in the Palais Abdelleya galleries in Tunis.

But an embarrassed religious establishment decided it was the popularity of the Left that needed to be punished. First on the hit-lists were Chokri Belaid—a charismatic and secular leftist and a lawyer for civil liberties—and Mohamed Brahmi, a socialist who said he practiced his belief within his home, ruling out all political Islam as a viable path for the 21st century. Brahmi and Belaid were personalities who animated and rallied the loyalty of the lower classes towards the left and away from both Ennahda and more extremist forms of Muslim Brotherhood Islamism. They were both assassinated by young Salafis, leaving the country in shock and in mourning, and laying the path for the attacks on the Bardo museum (the museum that houses the antiquities of Carthage.) Even during the attacks on art galleries and the demand by offended religious people to have the right to censor and persecute Tunisian painters, Belaid had legally represented the animation film based Maryam Satrapi's Persepolis against government detractors in court—though defending Persepolis was only one small aspect of the political activities that would sentence him.

Rights of the Poor, Women's Rights Vs. Christian Neoliberalism and Chastity

The Tunisian rejection of market-power and regulation defended by Ennahda, revealed that for modern Islamism, the Koranic guide to the economy is precisely the aspect of Mohammed that was closest to an entrepreneur. Mohammed defended the right to make profit from trade as moral. Islamism and market-fundamentalism, thanks to the Saudi Arabian influence, has shown itself as a continuum in Tunisia. The rejection of Ennnahda's attempts at de-regulation led to some of the most interesting protests—from the point of view of the cause of the Arab woman—in 2013: protests erupted in Tunisia when Ennahda officials threatened to remove the state healthcare coverage for women's abortions.

Abortion of unwanted pregnancies is legally available in famously progressive Tunisia, and the operation covered by the state medical programs. Popular discontent was directed at how the "austerity-measure" would lead to the advantage for women of wealthy families, whereas a poorer woman would be unable to access the right to abort. The motion by a religious party, threatening not to illegalize abortion, but to stop state funding for the operation, led to a fascinating outbreak of public resistance showing how neoliberal economics inevitably leads to enforcing conservatism, even in Muslim countries in Africa.

The protests epitomized the goal of Arab participants in the revolts to have their uprisings on their own terms, and not stolen away by the global neoliberal market, as Western military and financial interests that inevitably found an unlikely ally in the Islamist religious right in the struggle to control the outcomes of the revolts.

The "Arab Spring" Began in Iraq 2003

Arguably, the very first "Arab Spring" transformation was not Tunis January 2010: it was Iraq 2003, as Bush-II and the NeoConservatives announced their liberation of Iraq from its secular regime, a dictatorship that committed innumerable crimes while also providing a welfare state and a controlled economy, comforting its people in a security provided by the oil. Saddam and Ghaddaffi both kept much of the national resources and institutes under a nationalized economy, not giving in to foreign demands they remained patriotic militarists. Benali did this to a much lesser extent, as his dynasty was less ideologically committed and flirted with the new

96

economic fashions of neoliberalism, as well as trying to keep up the image of the old authoritarian ways of Habib Bourghuiba. Tunisia's first ruler after independence, Bourghuiba appointed Benali as his gendarme, then as prime minister, and was overthrown by his own appointee in the so-called "Jasmine revolution", a military coup d'etat in November 1987. In a comical manner, the Western media coverage of the Tunisian revolt named the 2011 popular uprisings after the "Jasmine revolution", the coup waged by the overthrown authoritarian.

The ruthless assassinations of Belaid and Brahmi are wounds still deeply felt in the Tunisian society that has undergone a wave of paralysis and timidity after having lost some of the most courageous and vocal fighters for the small nation's sovereignty in an increasingly fragmented and alienated North African and Middle Eastern region.

What would have materialized as the single "success-story" (to use a typically capitalist phrase) among the countries of the Arab revolts of 2011, was prevented with the coordinated killings of those politicians. The left had regained the respect of the labouring classes and the unemployed. Until 2012, the communist parties were not taken as seriously among the Tunisian majority, as the political left was associated with a fashion of the 1970s and the identity politics of middle class intellectuals who drenched in nostalgia for that era. In the shadow of Ennahda's disappointment of the desires of its working class supporters, the left began to impress, to shine and bedazzle the people who it claimed represent—the "proletariat"—for the first time, instead of being satisfied with the enthusiasm of Tunis cosmopolitan intellectuals. Individuals such as Belaid and Brahmi, were those mostly likely to secure the revolution by the Tunisians, on their terms—and not Saudi Arabia's or Qatar's; not according to the plans of the United States. The dream was of securing the Tunisian revolution by playing, neither by the rules of Sarkozy nor those of Francois Hollande: the "lone success story" of the Arab revolts in Tunisia needed to be according the general, pluralistic will of the Tunisians towards an independent, post-authoritarian democracy. But with the anti-political assassinations—an act of "politicide"—this dream again stood subverted, as it was subverted in each and every case of the "Arab spring's" concert of the disillusioned, from Tripoli to Aleppo.

Today, under president Essebsi, the political structures of the Nidaa Tounes party use the rhetoric of counter-terrorism and "security". The Essebsi government has re-established many of the old, authoritarian surveillance structures, and the system of provincial deputies that was dismantled for having been staples of the Benali regime. Essebsi himself was part of Bourghuiba's circle and feeds on the still-extant sentimental love many Tunisians have for Habib Bourghuiba, "the Modernizer," a megalomaniacal dictator who appointed Benali as prime minister, and whose program for modernization of Tunisia involved the eradication of the Touareg bedouin ways of life in the South. The small North African country, has long lived in fear of the Algerian scenario of civil war's unlimited terrorism. Benali could always trust the people's fear of a situation far worse than dictatorship, which is civil war, as happened next-door in Algeria. With the reminiscent and nightmarish examples of Syria and Libya, the fear has returned, and the politics of fear in Arab countries often leads the people to trust a Leviathan-like dictator or authoritarian power who disciplines and who nannies, even by torture and surveillance, should the fear loom sufficiently large.
*

Publisher's list

If you have enjoyed *Ouafa and Thawra: About a Lover From Tunisia* **consider these other fine books from Mwanaka Media and Publishing:**

Cultural Hybridity and Fixity by Andrew Nyongesa
The Water Cycle by Andrew Nyongesa
Tintinnabulation of Literary Theory by Andrew Nyongesa
I Threw a Star in a Wine Glass by Fethi Sassi
South Africa and United Nations Peacekeeping Offensive Operations by Antonio Garcia
Africanization and Americanization Anthology Volume 1, Searching for Interracial, Interstitial, Intersectional and Interstates Meeting Spaces, Africa Vs North America by Tendai R Mwanaka
A Conversation..., A Contact by Tendai Rinos Mwanaka
A Dark Energy by Tendai Rinos Mwanaka
Africa, UK and Ireland: Writing Politics and Knowledge Production Vol 1 by Tendai R Mwanaka
Best New African Poets 2017 Anthology by Tendai R Mwanaka and Daniel Da Purificacao
Keys in the River: New and Collected Stories by Tendai Rinos Mwanaka
Logbook Written by a Drifter by Tendai Rinos Mwanaka
Mad Bob Republic: Bloodlines, Bile and a Crying Child by Tendai Rinos Mwanaka
How The Twins Grew Up/Makurire Akaita Mapatya by Milutin Djurickovic and Tendai Rinos Mwanaka
Writing Language, Culture and Development, Africa Vs Asia Vol 1 by Tendai R Mwanaka, Wanjohi wa Makokha and Upal Deb
Zimbolicious Poetry Vol 1 by Tendai R Mwanaka and Edward Dzonze
Zimbolicious: An Anthology of Zimbabwean Literature and Arts, Vol 3 by Tendai Mwanaka
Under The Steel Yoke by Jabulani Mzinyathi
A Case of Love and Hate by Chenjerai Mhondera
Epochs of Morning Light by Elena Botts
Fly in a Beehive by Thato Tshukudu
Bounding for Light by Richard Mbuthia

White Man Walking by John Eppel
A Cat and Mouse Affair by Bruno Shora
Sentiments by Jackson Matimba
Best New African Poets 2018 Anthology by Tendai R Mwanaka and Nsah Mala
Drawing Without Licence by Tendai R Mwanaka
Writing Grandmothers/ Escribiendo sobre nuestras raíces: Africa Vs Latin America Vol 2 by Tendai R Mwanaka and Felix Rodriguez
The Scholarship Girl by Abigail George
Words That Matter by Gerry Sikazwe
The Gods Sleep Through It All by Wonder Guchu
The Ungendered by Delia Watterson
The Big Noise and Other Noises by Christopher Kudyahakudadirwe
Tiny Human Protection Agency by Megan Landman
Ghetto Symphony by Mandla Mavolwane
Sky for a Foreign Bird by Fethi Sassi
A Portrait of Defiance by Tendai Rinos Mwanaka
When Escape Becomes the only Lover by Tendai R Mwanaka
Where I Belong: moments, mist and song by Smeetha Bhoumik
Nationalism: (Mis)Understanding Donald Trump's Capitalism, Racism, Global Politics, International Trade and Media Wars, Africa Vs North America Vol 2 by Tendai R Mwanaka
Of Bloom Smoke by Abigail George
Ashes by Ken Weene and Omar O Abdul
Ouafa and Thawra: About a Lover From Tunisia by Arturo Desimone
Thoughts Hunt The Loves/Pfungwa Dzinovhima Vadiwa by Jeton Kelmendi
وَالغَمَام...ويَسهَرُ اللَّيلُعَلَىشَفَتي by Fethi Sassi
A Letter to the President by Mbizo Chirasha
Righteous Indignation by Jabulani Mzinyathi:
This is Not a Poem by Richard Inya

Soon to be released

Notes From a Modern Chimurenga: Collected Stories by Tendai Rinos Mwanaka
Tom Boy by Megan Landman

My Spiritual Journey: A Study of the Emerald Tablets by Jonathan Thompson

Rhythm of Life by Olivia Ngozi Osouha

Blooming Cactus By Mikateko Mbambo

School of Love and Other Stories by Ricardo Felix Rodriguez

Cycle of Life by Ikegwu Michael Chukwudi

Denga reshiri yokunze kwenyika by Fethi Sassi

Because Sadness is Beautiful by Tanaka Chidora

PHENOMENOLOGY OF DECOLONIZING THE UNIVERSITY: Essays in the Contemporary Thoughts of Afrikology by Zvikomborero Kapuya

INFLUENCE OF CLIMATE VARIABILITY ON THE PREVALENCE OF DENGUE FEVER IN MANDERA COUNTY, KENYA by NDIWA JOSEPH KIMTAI

https://facebook.com/MwanakaMediaAndPublishing/

Printed in the United States
By Bookmasters